of
Archbishop
Oscar Romero

Compiled and introduced by
Don Mullan

a little book company

First published in 2005 by
a little book company
11 Hillsbrook Crescent, Perrystown,
Dublin 12, Ireland.
email: *info@alittlebookcompany.com*
website: *www.alittlebookcompany.com*
in association with The Institute of the Blessed Virgin
Mary (Canada). *www.ibvm.org*
and SalvAide, Ottawa, Canada. *www.salvaide.ca*

Designed & typeset by David Houlden, PageWorks
Cover Painting: 'Romero Vitral' by Isaías Mata, ASTAC,
El Salvador
Photographer: Mario Mata, ASTAC, El Salvador
Produced in Ireland and
Printed in Canada by WebCom
ISBN: 0-9547047-1-1

To all Salvadoran communities
who continue working for a better society
and
to all who gave their lives, fearlessly,
in defence of Human Rights

and to

Joan Overholt IBVM,
faithful supporter of
Loretto (Canada)–La Bermuda (El Salvador)
community twinning

Acknowledgements

The publisher and editor gratefully acknowledge permission to quote from the following: *The Church Is All of You: Thoughts of Archbishop Oscar Romero*, compiled and translated by James R. Brockman (Minneapolis: Winston Press, 1984); *Archbishop Oscar Romero: Voice of the Voiceless — The Four Pastoral Letters and Other Statements* (Maryknoll, N.Y.: Orbis Books, 1985); *Oscar Romero, The Violence of Love*, compiled and translated by James R. Brockman (Farmington, Pa.: Plough Publishing House, 1998); *La voz de los sin voz* (San Salvador: UCA Editores, 1987) March 19, 1980 interview, 461; *Archbishop Oscar Romero — A Shepherd's Diary*, Translated by Irene B. Hodgson (Copyright ©1993, *United States Catholic Conference, Inc., Washington, DC 20017*, Published by St Anthony Messenger Press, USA and Novalis, Canada); *Monsenor Romero — El pueblo es mi profeta* (Equipo de Educacion, Maiz, El Salvador), translated by the Romero Centre, Dublin, Ireland.

4

Author's Acknowledgements

Sincere thanks are owed to the following for their kind support and assistance with this publication: Sr Evanne Hunter, IBVM, NGO Representative at the United Nations, who first conceived the idea of this little book during a short meeting in New York in the winter of 2004. I am very grateful to her for her support and encouragement. I wish also to thank Sr Deirdre Mullan, Director, Mercy Global Concern, who introduced us. Mr Jorge Pena, Director, SalvAide, Ottawa, Canada, for his support and advice. Gary Burke, RIP, who departed this life on 7 March 2003; to Seamus Cashman who gave me the idea of the Little Book series; to Moya Mullan for her invaluable advice on text, my designer David Houlden and Yvonne Golding for secretarial services. Last but not least, my family: Margaret, Thérèse, Carl and Emma for their continued patience, understanding, kindness and love.

Introduction

Oscar Arnulfo Romero y Galdámez was born on August 15th, 1917 in Ciudad Barrios, San Miguel, El Salvador, the son of the local postmaster. At 13 he was apprenticed to a carpenter but a year later he entered a junior seminary to prepare for the priesthood. He studied in El Salvador and Rome and was ordained in 1942, aged 24.

Fr Romero spent the first 25 years of his ministry working as a parish priest and diocesan secretary in San Miguel. From 1970–1974 he was auxiliary bishop of San Salvador before becoming Bishop of the Santiago de Maria diocese, which included his birthplace. In 1977, he returned to San Salvador as the newly elected Archbishop.

These were momentous times in the history of all Latin America. In 1968, at Medellin, Colombia, the Latin American hierarchy gathered to discuss the implementation of the Second Vatican Council. A fundamental shift occurred at Medellin with many of the Bishops opting to support the movements for justice and human rights. Again, in 1979, they gathered at Puebla, Mexico, to discuss the 'option for the poor'. Conservative elements both within and outside the church opposed the new direction. Many religious who opted for the poor were branded 'communists'.

El Salvador was at the heart of this religious and political turmoil where over half of its peasants were landless. Nothing short of an agrarian revolution was required to end the repression of the masses. Fourteen Salvadoran families controlled over 60 percent of the arable land. The military and powerful interests abroad ruthlessly protected them. Torture and murder, sometimes massacres, by the military and officially sanctioned death squads were aimed at repressing political aspirations.

The ruling élite welcomed Oscar Romero's appointment as Archbishop of San Salvador in February 1977 because of his innate conservative and cautious nature. It was short lived. Following the murder of his friend, Fr Rutilio Grande, SJ, along with two parishioners in March 1977, Archbishop Romero responded by cancelling all Sunday masses in the archdiocese and, instead, invited the faithful to gather in the capital for one unified mass — 250,000 people attended. It was both symbolic and a sign of his resolve. Henceforth, Archbishop Romero's mission was firmly on the side of the multitudes of poor and voiceless who populated El Salvador.

In a homily two months after Fr Grande's murder he stated: 'The church is concerned about those who cannot speak, those who suffer, those who are tortured, those who are silenced. This is not getting involved in politics. But when politics begins to "touch the altar," the church has the right to speak.'

On February 17th, 1980 Archbishop Romero wrote to President Jimmy Carter requesting the United States to cease sending military equipment and advisers to the Salvadoran military. The day before his murder, he pleaded with the military to follow their conscience: 'No soldier is obliged to obey an order that is contrary to the will of God.' On the evening of March 24th, 1980, while celebrating mass in the chapel of the Divine Providence Hospital, a marksman's bullet murdered the Archbishop of San Salvador. But Oscar Romero never died. As a martyr and a prophet he has been resurrected in the Salvadoran people. There he lives forever.

Don Mullan
Dublin, Ireland
March 24, 2005

Quotations from

Archbishop
Oscar Romero

I DON'T BELIEVE IN DEATH

Frequently I have been threatened
with death. I should tell you that,
as a Christian, I don't believe in death
without resurrection. If they kill me,
I will be resurrected
in the Salvadoran people.

OUR STORY

Our story is a very old one.
It is Jesus' story that we, in all modesty,
are trying to follow.

FAITH

... faith lived out in isolation from life
is not true faith.

CONSCIENCE

... we must consciously follow
where our consciences lead us ....

GREAT FAITHFULNESS

I visited Saint Peter's Basilica
and close to the beloved altar
dedicated to St Peter ... I asked for great
faithfulness to my Christian faith
and the courage, should it be necessary,
to die as those martyrs did ....

COMMUNION OF LOVE

We can find the blood of our teachers,
workers and peasants together with
the blood of our preachers.
This is called communion of love.
How sad would it be if, in a country
where so horrendous crimes
are committed every day,
we did not find the preachers
as part of the victims.
These preachers are the testimony
of a Church immersed
in the problems of the people.

TRUST IN GOD

We are the small David
against the giant Goliath
who trusts his weapons,
his power and his money.
We trust in the name of God.

CALL TO CONVERSION

With respect to the classes
that have social, political
and economic power,
the church calls upon them,
before all else, to be converted,
to remember their very grave responsibility
to overcome disorder and violence
not by means of repression
but through justice
and the participation of ordinary people.

LISTEN TO HIM!

To those who hold economic power,
the Lord of the world says
they should not close their eyes selfishly ....
They should understand that only by
sharing in justice, with those who do not
have such power, can they co-operate
for the good of the country. [Only then]
will they enjoy the peace and happiness
that cannot come from wealth
accumulated at the expense of others.
Listen to him!

20

TRUE RECONCILIATION

... agricultural reforms
are a theological need.
The land of a country shouldn't be
in the hands of a few people.
It should belong to everybody.
The land is a sign of justice and
reconciliation. There won't be true
reconciliation between our people
and God until ...
all Salvadorans are happy
and benefit from it.

CONVERSION

The Bishops, the Pope
and all the Christian people
are required to follow
the path of conversion in this world
as lived by Christ.
The pastors shouldn't settle down
comfortably but strive for conversion
along with the people.

THE PROPHET HOSEA

Read the book of Hosea and you will see
how church preaching today
doesn't say enough [about injustice]
compared to the eloquence
of this prophet against kings, big and
powerful people, reproaching them
for their abuse and unfairness.

HYPOCRISY

The Lord doesn't like the religion
of Sunday masses and unfair weekdays.
Religion with a lot of praying
but hypocrisy in the heart
is not Christian.

TRUE PEACE

Peace is not the product
of terror and fear.
Peace is not the silence of cemeteries.
Peace is not the product of violence
and repression ....
True Peace
is only achieved through justice ...
by sharing fairly the richness
of our country among all Salvadoran
men and women.

INSPIRATION AND STRENGTH

It was the hour for vespers,
and the basilica was fully illuminated.
We heard the organ filling the air and the
choir of monks singing in Gregorian chant.
Knelling by the tomb of ... the great St Paul,
in that atmosphere of prayer
that was almost heavenly,
I felt stirring in my memory, in my heart,
in my love ... inspiration and strength.

PRAYER

In my homily ... I talked about ...
how I went to Puebla
as the representative of a diocese
that was praying,
and I emphasized this a great deal.
As I thanked them for their prayers
that I felt so strongly,
I asked them to continue praying
so that this would be the greatest strength
of our diocese: prayer.

BEING MORE

The absolutisation of wealth
holds out to persons the ideal
of 'having more' and to that extent
reduces interest in 'being more',
whereas the latter
should be the ideal for true progress,
both for the people as such
and for every individual.
The absolute desire of 'having more'
encourages the selfishness that destroys
communal bonds among
the children of God.

GOD'S LAMP

Know that you are God's lamp.
ight taken from the glowing face of Christ
to enlighten human faces,
the lives of peoples,
the complications and problems
that humans create in their history.
Feel obliged to speak,
to enlighten like the lamp in the night.
Feel compelled
to light up the darkness.

WHAT IS THE POINT?

What is the point in going to college,
getting a degree,
being a professional,
if the only aim
is to earn more and more money?

THE POWER OF THE GOSPEL

The church ... is always ready
to make use of the only power it possesses
— the power of the gospel —
to throw light on any kind of activity
that will better establish justice.

THE KINGDOM OF GOD

The church believes
in the kingdom of God
as a progressive change
from the world of sin to a world of love
and justice,
one that begins in this world
but has its fulfillment in eternity.

THE KINGDOM OF GOD

In Latin America, in El Salvador,
the church, like Jesus,
has to go on proclaiming the good news
that the kingdom of God is at hand,
especially for [those of] the great majority
who, in worldly terms,
[have] been estranged from it
— the poor, the low-income classes,
the marginalized.

THE HOLY SPIRIT

I am a fragile man
and I have limitations ....
My task as pastor is what St Paul says
to us today:
'Don't extinguish the Holy Spirit' ....
If [as an authoritarian] I carry on
as though I were the Holy Spirit
building the church
according to my own tastes,
I would be extinguishing the same
Holy Spirit.

THE VOICE OF THE VOICELESS

The church would betray its own love
for God and its fidelity to the gospel
if it stopped being
'the voice of the voiceless'.

FAITHFUL TO ITS MISSION

The church is respected, praised,
even granted privileges,
so long as it preaches eternal salvation
and does not involve itself
in the real problems of our world.
But if the church is faithful to its mission
of denouncing the sin
that brings misery to many,
then it is persecuted and calumniated,
it is branded as subversive and communist.

AN EASTER CHURCH

We Christians have not thoroughly
assimilated ourselves to Jesus Christ.
We divorce faith from life
(we content ourselves
with preaching the faith
or celebrating it liturgically,
but we do not put love and justice
into practice).
An Easter church ... ought to
be a church of conversion,
of a fundamental turning back to Christ —
whose mirror we should be.

WOMEN RELIGIOUS

The work of the women religious
in the archdiocese
is more providential each day.

PROPHETIC MISSION

... this is the risk of any prophetic mission
of the Church:
to be criticized even by your own people
and even to find yourself alone,
but able to feel the satisfaction
of having tried
to be faithful to the gospel.

DUTY

The Church that fulfills its duty
cannot exist without being persecuted.

LET US BE WORTHY

Let us be worthy of this hour.

A GREAT DESIRE

Out of a great desire
to briefly see my dear town ...
I [visited] Ciudad Barrios ....
The memory of my infancy,
the contact with old friends,
renews in my life
my enthusiasm to continue the vocation
God gave me in [that] humble town ....
When I got back, I felt a little ill;
I think I am getting the flu.

TRADITION IS NOT A MUSEUM

To remain anchored
in a none-evolving traditionalism,
whether out of ignorance or selfishness,
is to close one's eyes to what is meant
by authentic Christian tradition.
The tradition that Christ
entrusted to his church is not a museum
of souvenirs to be protected.
It is true that tradition
comes out of the past ...
but it has always a view to the future.

THE VIRGIN MARY

I spoke ... in the spirit of Puebla
of how devotion to the Virgin
is a part of our Latin American identity,
but it is a devotion
which should be up-to-date ....
Mary ... is the inspiration for our suffering
people not in a passive way ...
but ... with the spiritual energy...
to transform injustice into an order
which is more humane and just.

POPE PAUL VI

The principal ideas ...
of Pope Paul VI's words ... [to me] were:
'I understand your difficult work.
It is a work that can be misunderstood;
it requires a great deal of patience
and a great deal of strength.
I already know that
not everyone thinks like you do ....
Nevertheless, proceed with courage,
with patience, with strength, with hope.'

DISUNITY

Our communities pointed out
that when disunity affects the hierarchy
and the clergy,
there results even greater confusion
among the people of God.
This is indeed true and,
faced with this evidence,
one can only be repentant,
reflect and exhort.

UNITY

... if I am the cause of any obstacle to ...
unity with my dear brother bishops ...
then I am willing to fix that ....
Unity is one of the fruits
of the Holy Spirit and ...
the people many times
interpret this Spirit
better than the hierarchy itself does.

AN EQUAL

I don't pretend to be anything other
than a Christian bishop.
A Christian who is carrying out his task
as a sign of unity.
I am not more than anybody else.

WHAT THE SPIRIT IS SAYING

If I were a zealous person
like those in the Gospel ...
I would say it is forbidden
for anyone to speak —
only I, the bishop, am allowed to speak.
No, I have to listen
to what the spirit is saying
through God's people
and then analyze it with them
and together use it to build the church.

HUMILITY

Be humble,
don't pretend to be humble.

DANGEROUS ACCUSATIONS

The morning newspapers ...
carried a full-page text
of Bishop Aparicio's homily ....
It is a strong condemnation of his priests.
He says that he cannot defend them
and almost accuses them himself,
exposing them to possible assassination ....
We have met with other priests
who are very angry
about such dangerous accusations.

ACCUSATIONS

Bishop Rivera came to see me
and we talked about the secret document
of denunciation the other four bishops
are preparing.
In it, they denounce me to the Holy See
in matters of faith, say I am politicized,
accuse me of promoting a pastoral work
with erroneous theological grounding ....

ACCUSATIONS

[They make] ... a whole series
of accusations that completely impugn
my ministry as a bishop.
I acknowledge my deficiencies before God,
but I believe that I have worked with
goodwill and that I am not guilty
of the serious things
of which they accuse me.

SOLIDARITY

I went to participate in the concelebration
with my brother bishops in ... San Miguel.
I noted in the bishops the ...
desire to marginalize me.
The people, on the other hand,
gave me a warm ovation ....
I do not feel any vanity, but rather
joy in my harmony with a people
who expect from their ... pastors
an increasingly deep solidarity.

ACCUSATIONS

Tonight Father Gregorio Rosa was with me
and we talked a great deal about the
accusations in the document
prepared by the other bishops
and about the reality of our archdiocese.
We are not going to answer it,
except through our actions
as we continue the pastoral work
of our archdiocese.

AT THE HOUR OF DEATH

We must save not the soul
at the hour of death
but the person living in history.

PAPAL AUDIENCE

I went again to the Prefecture ...
to try to get ... an audience
with the Holy Father.
I am very concerned
about the attitude they show
to the pastor of a diocese ....
They keep delaying the response
and I am afraid that
they are not going to grant the audience ....

PAPAL AUDIENCE

The Holy Father received me ....
When I took out the folder of reports ...
he smiled, seeing how thick it was ...
I also gave him … a photograph
of Father Octavio [Ortiz], ...
and extensive information
on his murder ....
He acknowledged that pastoral work
is very difficult in a political climate ....
He reminded me of his situation
in Poland ....

PAPAL AUDIENCE

I left, pleased by the meeting,
but worried to see how much
the negative reports ... of my pastoral work
had influenced him,
although deep down I remembered
that he had recommended
'courage and boldness',
but, at the same time, tempered
with the necessary prudence and balance.

PAPAL AUDIENCE

I have learned that one cannot expect
always to get complete approval
and that it is more useful to hear criticism
that can be used to improve our work.

THE POPE'S JUDGMENTS

[In Rome] the Pope asked Father Arrupe
[Superior General of the Jesuits]
specifically about me ....
Arrupe praised my pastoral work
[and] preaching.
It appears this influenced the Pope's
judgments. He noticed the Holy Father
was surprised when ... told
[that] six priests have been assassinated ....
it makes us think they do not give the Pope
objective reports on ... the Church
in our country.

ENCOURAGEMENT

I [met] two sisters who had been deported
to Guatemala and allowed to return.
The Minister has said that ...
their work is not of a religious nature.
The sisters asked for concrete examples ...
and none was offered ....
I ... encouraged them
to continue with their work,
always basing it on truth ...
because they are doing a great deal of good
in the remote village of Arcatao ....

I ENCOURAGED THEM

... a meeting of ex-priests ... told me
of their plan to create
a Christian base community.
I encouraged them in this objective,
since the fact that they have left the ministry
does not mean that they have stopped
being members of the Church.

OPTION FOR THE POOR

Because the church
has opted for the truly poor,
not for the fictitiously poor,
because it has opted for those
who really are oppressed and repressed,
the church lives in a political world,
and it fulfills itself as church
also through politics.
It cannot be otherwise if the church,
like Jesus,
is to turn itself toward the poor.

SOLIDARITY WITH THE POOR

... the church ... ought to be
in solidarity with the poor,
running the risks they run,
enduring the persecution that is their fate,
ready to give the greatest possible testimony
to its love by defending and promoting
those who were first in Jesus' love.

THE SALVADORAN OLIGARCHY

Let us put an end to the ... domination
of the Salvadoran oligarchy ...
afraid of losing control over investments,
agricultural exportation
and their monopoly of the land.
They defend their interests ... not using
the reason of popular support, but
with the only thing they have: money.
This money allows them buy
weapons and pay mercenaries
that kill the people and destroy
all calls for justice and freedom.

THE PREFERENCE OF JESUS

The spirit of the Lord has been given to me,
for he has anointed me.
He has sent me to bring the good news
to the poor, to proclaim liberty to captives
and to the blind new sight,
to set the downtrodden free,
to proclaim the Lord's year of favor
(Luke 4:18–19).

This preference of Jesus for the poor stands
out throughout the gospel.

JESUS' PREFERENCE

The church should share Jesus' preference
for those who have been used
for others' interests
and have not been in control
of their own destinies.

STRUCTURAL VIOLENCE

Structural violence ... takes concrete form
in the unjust distribution of wealth
and of property — especially insofar as it
includes landownership —
and, more generally, in that amalgam
of economic and political structures
by which the few grow
increasingly rich and powerful,
while the remainder
grow increasingly poor and weak.

STARVATION WAGES

Still today many industrial or transnational
corporations base their ability
to compete in international markets
on what they call 'low labor costs',
which in reality means starvation wages.

VIOLENCE

Those responsible for
the institutionalization of violence,
and for the international structures that
cause it, are those who monopolize
economic power instead of sharing it,
those 'who defend them through violence.'

REVOLUTIONS OF DESPAIR

Not a single victim
comes from the landowning class,
whereas those from among the *campesino*
population abound.
Faced with this oppression and repression,
there arises naturally
what Medellin called the
'explosive revolutions of despair'.

REPRESSION

The ruling class, especially the rural élite,
cannot allow unions
to be organized among ... laborers
so long as, from a capitalist point of view,
they believe their economic
interests are at risk.
This makes repression ... necessary
in order to maintain
and increase profit levels,
[despite] the growing poverty
of the working class.

INTIMIDATION

Mother Juanita came to tell me about
an attempt to set fire
to the convent at Tamanique.
Gasoline had been poured on the doors
and a fire had been started, but,
thank God, it was controlled in time.

THREATS

I told ... Father George ... I had received
telephone calls, threatening me
with death and a card with the swastika ...
ordering me to ... praise the members
of the security forces who have been killed
... and that if I do not do what they say,
they will kill me. I understand these
to be psychological threats.

PROTECTION

The secretary of the Ministry of Defense ...
came to see me and told me that he had
talked with the President,
the Minister and other men in
the government about the danger I am in,
and that they are offering me whatever
protection I want, even a bulletproof car.

PROTECTION

I thanked him ... saying respectfully that
I cannot accept this protection since
I want to run the same risks
as the people do.
I took the opportunity to ask him,
rather, to protect the people
in certain zones where ...
the military operations do so much damage
— or at least create so much terror.

PSYCHOSIS

After Mass, we went to visit
Father Grande's tomb in El Paisnal ....
The fear ... was noticeable.
The people watched from a distance,
but they did not come near.
An 'ear', as we say, was very close,
watching what we were doing.
In summary ... a psychosis has been created
in all these places so tormented
by the repression.

THE POOR AGAINST THE POOR

... policemen who die are also victims
of the injustice of our system ...
because policemen, labourers
and peasants all belong to the poor class.
The evil of the system is to put
the poor against the poor.

STOP THE REPRESSION

Brothers, you are from the same people;
you kill your fellow peasant.
No soldier is obliged to obey an order
that is contrary to the will of God.
In the name of God then, in the name
of this suffering people I ask you,
I beg you, I command you ...
stop the repression.

VIOLENCE

The church cannot refrain
from speaking out.
It can in no way reject what Jesus said:
'The kingdom of heaven
has been subjected to violence
and the violent are taking it by storm'
(Matt. 11:12).

VIOLENCE

Normally speaking,
violence is not part of human nature.
Persons do not find self-fulfillment
in humiliating, harming, kidnapping,
torturing or killing others.
Violence has other roots
which have to be exposed.

TURN THE OTHER CHEEK

The gospel's advice to turn the other cheek
to an unjust aggressor,
far from being passivity and cowardice,
is evidence of great moral strength
that can leave an aggressor
morally defeated and humiliated.

TORTURE

We talked with ... one of those who had
disappeared who escaped form jail.
He ... told us about horrible things
that happen in the mysterious realm
of the jails of the security forces where,
I am sure, are several people
we mourn as disappeared.
It is a very sensitive secret;
some really dreadful revelations!

REVENGE

My brother, Gaspar,
who holds an important post in ANTEL
[the state-owned telephone company],
has been unexpectedly demoted.
Without a doubt, this is revenge
on the government's part
because he is a relative of mine.
I am sorry that my family
is suffering as a result of
the prophetic task I must carry out.

DISAPPEARED

At my residence a suffering mother
was waiting for me,
along with her son's wife,
to tell me that her son,
a fifth-year medical student,
has disappeared.
She shared her story with me
and I understood the depth of her pain
and promised to do everything I could.
Tomorrow in the Mass
I will mention this new case of injustice.

RADIO MINISTRY

Yesterday I traveled
to Dulce Nombre de Maria
and the humble people of the countryside
told me how they had listened
to my words [on radio]
and how these words had helped them
to find consolation and help.
On hearing this I felt like weeping ....

BOMB

They awakened me
with an urgent telephone call ...
to tell me that a bomb had gone off
in the base of the YSAX [radio] transmitter
and that it has been completely destroyed ...
I am glad that the damages
were only of a material nature
that can be repaired ....

PLOTS

Tonight at ... around eleven o'clock,
another bomb exploded
in the library of the [Jesuit]
University of Central America.
Obviously these are plots of the extreme
right against the voice of the Church
and against the calls for social justice ....

ABUSE

What worries me
is the insensitivity being shown.
Little mountain towns are searched,
as are people's houses.
People are abused, disappear,
and all this happens as though it were
the most natural thing in the world.

HISTORICAL MOMENT

The changeable circumstances
in our history have made us better
understand the meaning of a transcendent,
but always pilgrim, church,
alert,
always seeking to apply the unique
and eternal gospel to
the historical moment it is living through.

NATIONAL SECURITY

I have already drawn attention ...
to the doctrine ... of national security as
the ideological foundation for repression.
Puebla frequently denounced
this new form of idolatry,
which has already been installed
in many Latin American countries ...
substantially it is identical with
that described at Puebla:

NATIONAL SECURITY

'In many instances
the ideologies of National Security
have helped to intensify the totalitarian
or authoritarian character of governments
based on the use of force,
leading to the abuse of power
and the violation of human rights.
In some instances they presume
to justify their positions with a
subjective profession of Christian faith.'

TO SPEAK THE TRUTH

To speak the truth is to suffer the interior
torment of the prophets.
Because it is much easier to preach lies,
adapt one's self to different situations
so as not to lose the upper hand,
to always have
flattering friends and power.

NEW EYES TO SEE

... the words of Exodus have ... finally
resounded in our ears:
'The cry of ... Israel has come to me
and I have witnessed the way in which
the Egyptians oppress them' (Exodus. 3:9).
These words have given us new eyes to see
what has always been the case among us,
but which has so often been hidden,
even from the view of the church itself.

EVERYDAY REALITIES

Amos and Isaiah are not just voices
from distant centuries;
their writings are not merely texts
that we reverently read in the liturgy.
They are everyday realities.
Day by day we live out the cruelty
and ferocity they denounced.

EVERYDAY REALITIES

We live them out when the mothers and
wives of those who have been arrested
or who have disappeared come to us,
when mutilated bodies turn up
in secret cemeteries, when those who fight
for justice and peace are assassinated.

MASTERS OF THEIR OWN LIBERATION

The world of the poor teaches us
that liberation will arrive
only when the poor are not simply
on the receiving end of handouts
from governments or from the church,
but when they themselves are
the masters of, and protagonists in,
their own struggle and liberation,
thereby unmasking the root
of false paternalism,
including ecclesiastical paternalism.

FREEDOM

There is no freedom to do evil.

LIBERATION

The overall plan of the liberation
proclaimed by the church
involves the whole person,
in all dimensions, including openness
to the absolute
that is God ....

TRUE LIBERATION

We raise up our prayer
to the Lord of history because,
'Unless the LORD build the house,
they labor in vain who build it …'
(Psalm 127:1).
Hate and vengeance can never be
the path to true liberation.
The road that leads to genuine well-being
always goes through justice and love.

THE VOICE OF JUSTICE

Nobody can kill the voice of justice.

A DEBT OF LOVE

There is a Spanish saying,
'Love must be paid with love.'
And that is the purpose of my pastoral
message: to repay a debt of love.
I have no other reason to be here.

THE GIFT OF LIFE

I celebrated ... the sixtieth wedding
anniversary of ... Don Francisco Ayala
and Doña Herminia ...
it made a lovely combination ...
to talk about the Virgin Mary,
the sanctity of marriage and faithfulness,
the gift of life
and the blessing of children ....
Shaking hands with everyone,
left in me the peacefulness of being rooted
in and loved by a people who know
how to return that love.

LOVE LIVES FOREVER

All power, all triumphs, all selfish
materialism, all the false successes of life
will pass with the world's form.
What does not pass away is love ...
the joy of sharing and of feeling that
we are all one family does not pass away.
In the evening of life
we will be judged by love.

I LOVE ALL

I love all and it is my mission
to love all ....
My heart excludes nobody.
I wish to say this frankly.

LOVE FOR OTHERS

No one is more alone than the selfish ....
If you give your life out of love for others ...
you will reap a great harvest.

SIN

The church, like Jesus, has to go on
denouncing sin in our own day.
It has to denounce the selfishness
that is hidden in everyone's heart,
the sin that dehumanizes persons,
destroys families and turns money,
possessions, profit and power into the
ultimate ends for which persons strive.

SIN

Let us remind ourselves
of a fundamental datum
of our Christian faith:
sin killed the Son of God,
and sin is what goes on killing
the children of God.
It is impossible to offend God without
offending one's brother or sister.

THE DENIAL OF GOD

And the worst offense against God,
the worst form of secularism,
as one of our Salvadoran theologians
has said, is:
To turn children of God,
temples of the Holy Spirit,
the body of Christ in history,
into victims of oppression and injustice,
into slaves to economic greed,
into fodder for political repression ...
the visible presence of the denial of God.

UNITED IN LOVE

God ... did not give us a social nature so
that we should destroy ourselves in
mutually hostile organizations,
but so that we could complement
our individual limitations
with the strength of all, united in love.

FALSE ADORATION

We have said [many] times that
the Church defends this right of people
to organize. [However], although the
original purpose may be noble,
it may turn into false adoration when the
organization is considered as the supreme
factor and all the interests of the people
are subordinated to the interests
of the organization.

FUNDAMENTALISM

It is harmful to become so radical
and place oneself at such an extreme
as to think 'Only what I do is good'.
Already there are movements in religious
life that want to take possession
of the monopoly of Christ, the Holy Spirit.

UNITY

A healthy pluralism is necessary.
We don't want everybody to be the same ....
Unity means plurality.

A SERVANT OF THE PEOPLE

There was a great deal of applause
during the homily ... in the basilica ....
I explained that this does not
make me swell up with pride;
that, rather, [it makes] me feel
more of a servant of the people ....
I asked them to be very committed
to prayers and to following
Christ with his cross.

TITLES

St Teresa of Avila once spoke
of how confused we all become
about titles for the hierarchy:
yes, your Excellency; yes, your Eminence.
It is difficult to understand it all,
it all seems so clownish:
'Your Excellence! Your Excellence!',
all the time. How much more simple
and beautiful is the name Christian!

SAY NO WHEN YOU HAVE TO

As a Christian you should use your own
criterion to know how to say
no when you have to.
Do not follow the rest when they do what
they shouldn't be doing as Christians.

A GREAT FRIEND

I went to the funeral of Don Marcel Weil,
a great Jewish friend from way back ...
at whose house I feel at home ...
he was a man who respected
each person's faith; and his personal
honesty is truly a guarantee
that God has received him in heaven.

TRUE RELIGION

God is spirit. He does not need a temple.
The temple of Jerusalem had
a relative significance,
like all the temples of the world.
The church ... as Christ said ...
looks for people who adore God
in spirit and truth.
This can be done under a tree,
on a mountain or by the sea.
Wherever there maybe an honest heart
which truly looks for God,
there is true religion.

GENUINE LAWS

With regard to the lack of protection
for those who need it most,
let us recall that genuine laws
were made to protect the weakest,
those, who without the law,
are prey to the powerful.

THE NOBEL ART OF POLITICS

Those who are suited
or can become suited
should prepare themselves
for the difficult,
but at the same time,
the very noble art of politics.
[They] should seek to practice this art
without regard for their own interests
or for material advantages.

PRAY FOR THOSE WHO PERSECUTE YOU

The church has never incited
to hatred or revenge,
not even at those saddest of moments
when priests have been murdered
and faithful Christians have been killed
or have disappeared ....
On the contrary,
it has recalled the command,
'pray for those who persecute you'
(Matt. 5.44).

A SURE REWARD

We know that no one can go on forever,
but those who have put into their work
a sense of very great faith, of love of God,
of hope among human beings,
find it all results in the splendors of
a crown that is the sure reward
of those who labor thus,
cultivating truth, justice, love
and goodness on the earth.

TO GIVE ONE'S LIFE

To give life to the poor one has to give of
one's own life, even to give one's life itself.
'A man can have no greater love than
to lay down his life for his friends'
(John 15:13).

DO NOT FEAR

Do not remain passive
for fear of sacrifice
and personal risks.
All audacious and truly effective acts
involve some kind of risks.
If you remain passive, you will also be
responsible for injustice
and its consequences ....

THE SPIRIT OF MARTYRDOM

Giving your life is not only being killed.
Giving your life, having the spirit of
martyrdom is giving in responsibility,
in silence, in prayer.
Giving your life is
the honest fulfillment of duty,
in the silence of daily life,
like the mother who,
without making a great fuss ...
gives birth, feeds the baby,
brings it up
and takes care of it with love.

MUCH REMAINS TO BE DONE

There are still many questions
waiting to be answered.
Much thinking remains to be done.
We must do it together,
pastors and people of God,
never separated
from our union in Christ.
We must do it in the light of our faith
and of the social situation
of our country.

The Little Book of Archbishop Oscar Romero has been
produced in association with:

INSTITUTE OF THE BLESSED VIRGIN MARY (IBVM), CANADA

The Institute of the Blessed Virgin Mary (IBVM), also known as
the Loretto Sisters, was founded by Mary Ward (1585–1645),
as a community of women, who, freed from the confines of the
cloister, could respond to the needs of their time. Today, IBVM
Sisters, world-wide, commit themselves to promoting dignity
and liberation for all — especially women and children;
challenging unjust systems and structures; standing with those
on the fringes of society; and showing reverent care for the
earth and all creation. Loretto (Canada) recently celebrated
the 15th anniversary of twinning with the community of
Marianella Garcia Villas in La Burmuda, El Salvador.
www.ibvm.org

SALVAIDE

Founded in 1985, SalvAide is a Canadian-based charitable
non-governmental organization that supports sustainable
development initiatives in El Salvador.
Phone: (613) 233 6215. *www.salvaide.ca*

CARRANZA BARRISTERS & SOLICITORS
www.carranza.on.ca/

CENTER FOR EXCHANGE AND SOLIDARITY (CIS)
www.cis-elsalvador.org